Made in United States
Orlando, FL
08 December 2021

11305946R00061